50 Delicious Cauliflower Recipes

(50 Delicious Cauliflower Recipes - Volume 1)

Alice Tinsley

Copyright: Published in the United States by Alice Tinsley/ © ALICE TINSLEY

Published on December, 07 2020

All rights reserved. No part of this publication may be reproduced, stored in retrieval system, copied in any form or by any means, electronic, mechanical, photocopying, recording or otherwise transmitted without written permission from the publisher. Please do not participate in or encourage piracy of this material in any way. You must not circulate this book in any format. ALICE TINSLEY does not control or direct users' actions and is not responsible for the information or content shared, harm and/or actions of the book readers.

In accordance with the U.S. Copyright Act of 1976, the scanning, uploading and electronic sharing of any part of this book without the permission of the publisher constitute unlawful piracy and theft of the author's intellectual property. If you would like to use material from the book (other than just simply for reviewing the book), prior permission must be obtained by contacting the author at author@shellfishrecipes.com

Thank you for your support of the author's rights.

Content

50 AWESOME CAULIFLOWER RECIPES. 4

1. Aloo Gobi ~ A Dry Indian Curry Of Cauliflower, Potato & Peas 4
2. Andy Bennett's Creamy Cauliflower Pasta Carbonara 4
3. Bacon Y Cauliflower Gratin 5
4. Caramelized Cauliflower With Tahini 6
5. Cauliflower Couscous 7
6. Cauliflower Fritters 7
7. Cauliflower Pasta 7
8. Cauliflower Potato Soup 8
9. Cauliflower Roast With A Nod To Ina 9
10. Cauliflower Soup 9
11. Cauliflower Soup With Coconut Milk & Chillies 9
12. Cauliflower And Mushroom Gratin 10
13. Cauliflower, Brussels Sprouts & Crimini Sauté 11
14. Cauliflower, Snap Peas And Tomato Salad 11
15. Cheesy Cauliflower Casserole 12
16. Creamy Cauliflower Puree With Fenugreek 12
17. Creamy Roasted Cauliflower Soup 12
18. Crispy Parmesan Cauliflower Tots 13
19. Curried Cauliflower Flatbread 13
20. Curried Mustard Chickpeas And Cauliflower 14
21. Garlic Roasted Potato And Spinach (or Cauliflower) Curry 14
22. Genius Cauliflower Soup From Paul Bertolli 15
23. Harissa Cauliflower With Mint And Aleppo Pepper 15
24. Ina Garten's Cauliflower Toasts 16
25. Indian Stuffed Cauliflower Chappati (Gobi Ka Paratha) 16
26. Korean Fried Cauliflower 17
27. Lentil Salad With Roasted Radicchio & Cauliflower 18
28. Macaroni Cauliflower And Cheese 19
29. Mushroom Pilaf With Cauliflower Rice 19
30. Mustard & Cheddar Roasted Cauliflower . 20
31. Pizza With Roasted Cauliflower, Calabrian Chiles And Green Olive Tapenade 20
32. ROASTED CAULIFLOWER WITH SMOKED PAPRIKA 21
33. Red Pepper And Cauliflower Chowder 21
34. Roast Cauliflower With Raisins And Parsley Dressing 22
35. Roasted Cauliflower & Avocado Salad For New Parents 22
36. Roasted Cauliflower And Potatoes With Bengali Spices 23
37. Roasted Cauliflower With Lemony, Garlicky And Capers Dressing 23
38. Roasted Cauliflower With Spaghetti Squash And Crisp Prosciutto 24
39. Roasted Cauliflower With Tahini And Lemon 24
40. Roasted Curried Cauliflower In A Mustard Thyme Cream Sauce 25
41. Rustic Cauliflower Bake 25
42. Sassy Moussaka With Cauliflower Parsnip Puree 26
43. Sauteed Tri Color Cauliflower 26
44. Smoky Roasted Cauliflower And Celery Root Soup 27
45. Squash And Cauliflower Salad With Cranberry Beans And Salsa Verde 27
46. Sweet And Sour Stir Fry With Cauliflower Rice 28
47. Turmeric Roasted Cauliflower With Activated Charcoal And Goji Berries 28
48. Vegan Cauliflower Alfredo Sauce 29
49. Whipped Cauliflower 30
50. Cauliflower Shiitake Soup With Truffle Oil 30

INDEX 32
CONCLUSION 34

50 Awesome Cauliflower Recipes

***

1. Aloo Gobi ~ A Dry Indian Curry Of Cauliflower, Potato & Peas

Serving: Serves 2-4 | Prep: | Cook: | Ready in:

Ingredients

- 2 medium potatoes, peeled and cubed
- 1/2 medium cauliflower, cut into florets
- 1 cup peas
- 2 tablespoons oil
- 1/2 teaspoon brown mustard seeds
- 1/2 teaspoon cumin seeds
- 1 tablespoon Arvinda's Madras Masala
- 1 teaspoon salt
- 1/4 cup cilantro, finely chopped, to garnish
- 1/2 teaspoon Arvinda's Garam Masala, to garnish (optional)

Direction

- Heat oil in large pot on medium heat. Add mustard and cumin seeds. Fry until they sizzle and mustard seeds pop.
- Add potatoes, cauliflower and peas. Sprinkle in Arvinda's Madras Masala and salt. Mix.
- Cover pot and cook on low heat until potatoes are tender and cooked. Remove in a serving dish and garnish with Arvinda's Garam Masala and cilantro. Serve with another Indian curry, flatbread and rice.

2. Andy Bennett's Creamy Cauliflower Pasta Carbonara

Serving: Serves 2 | Prep: 0hours20mins | Cook: 0hours30mins | Ready in:

Ingredients

- Pasta Carbonara
- 1 tablespoon (12g) olive oil
- 1 cup (100g) sliced spring onions or green onions
- 2 tablespoons (20g) roughly chopped garlic
- 1 cup (200g) Creamy Cauliflower Sauce (from below)
- 2 cups dried pasta, (250g) cooked al dente pasta (from about 125g dry pasta—for the rigatoni we used, this was about 2 cups dry pasta)
- 2/3 cup (90g) fresh or frozen green peas, cooked in salted water
- 1/2 cup Scant, (10g) chopped flat-leaf parsley
- 6 tablespoons (12g) finely grated Parmesan
- Smoked sea salt, to taste (optional)
- Freshly ground black pepper, to taste
- 1 tablespoon (4g) toasted breadcrumbs, or more to taste
- Creamy Cauliflower Sauce
- 2 cups (200g) cauliflower florets (in roughly 1/2-inch pieces)
- 2 1/4 cups (500g) vegetable stock or broth
- 1/2 cup (100g) olive oil
- Salt to taste

Direction

- Pasta Carbonara
- Heat the olive oil in a large sauté pan over medium heat. Add the spring onions and cook, stirring occasionally, until softened, about 2 minutes. Add the garlic and cook until the onions and garlic are turning light golden. Add the sauce, pasta, and peas and heat everything through, stirring occasionally, about 2 minutes.

- Once hot, stir in the cheese and parsley, season with smoked salt and black pepper to taste and place in a serving bowl. Sprinkle with bread crumbs and serve immediately.
- Creamy Cauliflower Sauce
- In a medium saucepan, cover the cauliflower with vegetable stock and simmer, partially covered, until really tender, about 20 minutes. Blend the cauliflower and stock till smooth with a blender or hand blender. While the blender is running, slowly pour in olive oil to emulsify.
- Store any leftovers airtight in the refrigerator and use as a creamy sauce, warm or cold.

3. Bacon Y Cauliflower Gratin

Serving: Serves 4 - 6 | Prep: | Cook: | Ready in:

Ingredients

- 1 cup bread crumbs, freshly made from bread that's a few days old (artisanal or sandwich, whatever you have)
- 3 slices really good bacon
- Sea salt
- 1 small cauliflower, including core and stems
- 1 teaspoon chopped fresh marjoram leaves
- 3 cloves of garlic, peeled and smashed
- Tiny pinch of ground cloves
- 3 eggs
- 1/2 cup sharp feta, crumbled
- 1/2 cup ricotta, preferably homemade
- 1/2 cup heavy cream
- 1 teaspoon fresh thyme leaves
- 2-3 tablespoons chopped Italian parsley
- Black pepper to taste
- 2 tablespoons finely grated Pecorino Romano or Parmigiano
- Butter for the gratin dish (and an extra 2-3 tablespoons for the topping, if you are making this well in advance)

Direction

- If you are making breadcrumbs for this dish, do it now and set them aside, but don't bother to wash out the bowl of your food processor.
- Heat your oven to 375 degrees F and generously butter a medium large gratin dish. (If it's a bit on the large size, all the better. This will allow for more crispy crumbs on the greater surface area!)
- In a large skillet for which you have a good tight lid, cook the bacon over medium heat until it's a nice mahogany color. Drain the slices on a paper towel and pour off all of the fat, except about 1 tablespoon, into a small bowl or jar. Keep it near the stove, as you'll need it soon. Do not wipe out the skillet.
- While the bacon is cooking, prepare the cauliflower by cutting off the florets. Keep them separate as you cut the stems into one-inch pieces. They are more dense, requiring more time to soften, so they need to be cooked separately at first.
- Once you've removed the bacon, put the cauliflower stems into the skillet, given them a good stir, add a pinch of salt, and cook over medium heat, stirring frequently, for a few minutes. Add a little water – about ¼ cup – and put the lid on. Set your timer for 4 minutes, but check about half way through, stirring the stems around just a bit and putting the cover back on without delay. They should be getting a light brown glaze from the bacon drippings and small bits left in the skillet. If the pan seems too dry, add a bit more water but immediately put the cover back on.
- After another minute or so, add the cauliflower florets, garlic, cloves (garlic's best friend) and fresh marjoram; stir well. Add ½ cup of water and cover the skillet. Let it cook for about five minutes, checking quickly after 2, and adding a bit more water if it seems dry.
- While the cauliflower is cooking, cut the cooled, crisp bacon into ½" squares. After the cauliflower has cooked for 5 minutes, remove the lid. If there is a lot of liquid in the bottom, reduce it by turning up the heat to cook it for a minute or so, stirring frequently.

- Set aside 12 or 15 of the larger floret pieces. This is optional. I like a bit of textural variety in dishes like this, but if you want to skip this detail, that's fine.
- Put all of the remaining cooked cauliflower, garlic, cloves and marjoram into a food processor, scraping the skillet well to get all of the little pieces. Pulse firmly five or six times. Scrape down the sides and pulse a few more times. You want to mash it all up well, but not to make a puree. Allow it to cool for a few minutes, stirring occasionally to facilitate that.
- Heat the skillet over a medium flame and pour at least two tablespoons of bacon fat back into it. Add the bread crumbs and cook for about a minute, stirring constantly to coat well. Add about 2/3 of the bacon pieces and stir well to incorporate.
- In a large bowl, whisk together the eggs, feta, ricotta, cream, thyme, nutmeg, parsley and black pepper, along with the remaining 1/3 of the bacon pieces. Add the mashed vegetables from the food processor and stir well to combine. Gently fold in the reserved florets.
- Pour into the gratin dish; then sprinkle with the grated parmesan. Cover with the bacon-y bread crumbs.
- Bake on the middle shelf of your oven for 30 – 40 minutes, until the bread crumbs are a nice toasty brown. (If baking well in advance, so that you'll be refrigerating the dish, don't sprinkle on the bacon-y bread crumbs. Cover tightly with a lid or foil. Bake for about 30 minutes and let cool covered. Bring to room temperature before baking; sprinkle on the bread crumbs, bake in the upper third of your oven until the crumbs are brown. I usually drizzle extra butter on the crumbs, to help with the browning.
- I hope you enjoy this. ;o)

4. Caramelized Cauliflower With Tahini

Serving: Serves 3 | Prep: | Cook: |Ready in:

Ingredients

- 1 head of cauliflower, cleaned, leaves removed & cut into florets (about 4 cups)
- 1 small white onion, halved & sliced thinly (about 2 cups)
- 1 tablespoon extra virgin olive oil
- 4 tablespoons lemon juice
- 3 tablespoons minced garlic
- 2 teaspoons paprika
- 2 tablespoons parsley
- 1/2 teaspoon salt
- 1/2 teaspoon pepper
- 1/8 cup tahini

Direction

- Preheat oven 425 degrees F
- Place cauliflower in a single layer on a baking sheet lined with parchment paper
- Add 1/4 tsp each salt & pepper to cauliflower
- Bake cauliflower 15 minutes then turn on the broiler on high to cook another 5 minutes
- Remove cauliflower from oven & place aside
- While cauliflower is cooking, heat a medium pan to medium high
- Add extra virgin olive oil to the pan
- Once the oil is hot, add the onions to the pan
- Cook the onions until tender, stirring constantly
- The onions can burn fast so watch carefully & remove when tender 8-10 minutes otherwise they will burn
- Place onions on a paper towel & add 1/2 tsp salt & pepper
- To the pan you used to cook the onions, turn the heat to low & add minced garlic
- You should have enough oil left in the pan otherwise add a tiny bit more
- After a minute, turn heat off add lemon juice, paprika, 1 tbsp. parsley, tahini & whisk in 12

tbsp. warm water to thin (I added 12 tbsp. to mine)
- Be sure to continuously whisk the sauce as you're adding the water or it may burn
- Place cauliflower in a bowl, add onions to the top then spoon tahini over it (I like to reserve about half the sauce for dipping)
- Sprinkle remaining cauliflower on top & enjoy!

5. Cauliflower Couscous

Serving: Serves 4 | Prep: | Cook: | Ready in:

Ingredients

- 1/3 cup Pine Nuts
- 2 cloves Garlic, pressed
- 2 tablespoons Duck Fat, (or other choice of fat to saute), divided
- 2 Raw Carrot, medium, peeled and sliced
- 1 Yellow Bell Pepper, diced
- 1 cup Cherry Tomato, sliced
- 1 teaspoon Sea Salt
- 1/2 teaspoon Black Pepper, (25 grinds)
- 4 Green Onion, sliced
- 1/2 Lemon, wedges, for garnish
- 1 tablespoon Extra Virgin Olive Oil, for garnish
- 1/4 cup Flat Leaf Parsley, chopped, for garnish

Direction

- In a large skillet over medium heat, sauté the pine nuts and garlic in 1 Tbsp. of the duck fat. When the pine nuts are golden brown, remove them from the skillet and set aside. Add the remaining 1 Tbsp. of duck fat to the skillet and sauté the carrots, bell pepper, and tomatoes for about 15 minutes, until soft. Season with the salt and pepper.
- Grate the cauliflower with the stems parallel to the grating surface (giving you longer grains of "rice"). Add the cauliflower to the skillet along with the sliced scallions, toasted pine nuts, and garlic.
- Serve with a squeeze of lemon juice and a drizzle of olive oil, garnished with flat-leaf parsley.

6. Cauliflower Fritters

Serving: Serves makes about 2 dozen patties | Prep: | Cook: | Ready in:

Ingredients

- Boil until tender:
- 1 1/2 cups fresh or frozen cauliflower
- Mix together:
- 1 cup flour
- 1/2 cup grated romano
- 1 teaspoon black pepper
- 3/4 teaspoon garlic salt
- 2 eggs
- 2/3 cup water
- 1 teaspoon baking powder

Direction

- Add the cooked cauliflower to the batter and mix.
- Drop by tablespoon into a frying pan of hot oil.
- Cook on both sides at medium heat (about 4 min on each side).
- Remove to paper towel to drain.
- You can substitute seasonal vegetables for the cauliflower. Zucchini is also good.

7. Cauliflower Pasta

Serving: Serves 2 hungry people | Prep: | Cook: | Ready in:

Ingredients

- 6 garlic cloves
- 6-8 anchovy fillets (use up to the whole small tin of anchovies)
- 1/2 teaspoon red pepper flakes, or to taste
- salt and pepper to taste
- 4 tablespoons olive oil, plus extra for serving
- 2 tablespoons anchovy oil (from tin of anchovies), or oilve oil
- 1 Head of cauliflower
- 2 handfuls Thin spaghetti, or enough for two
- 2 tablespoons chopped fresh italian parsley (use dried to be cheaper if you have it on hand)
- optional, Parmesan cheese!

Direction

- Pre-heat oven to 450 degrees.
- Combine first 3 ingredients on a cutting board and roughly chop into a chunky paste. Season with salt and pepper.
- Put mixture into a large bowl, add oils (anchovy and olive).
- Cut florets off head of cauliflower. Add florets to the mixture and toss to combine.
- Place mixed florets onto a large rimmed baking sheet. Arrange evenly into a single layer.
- Place in oven and roast cauliflower until softened and slightly blackened on edges and tips, 25-30 minutes depending on oven strength.
- Meanwhile cook pasta according to package.
- Chop fresh Italian parsley and set aside.
- When the pasta and the cauliflower have finished cooking, add pasta to a large serving bowl and combing with roasted cauliflower mixture. Top with chopped parsley and drizzle olive oil on top to taste. Serve Parmesan cheese on the side if desired.
- Additional Options: Dish is also delicious (and higher in calories) when bacon is added. If you want to try this, fry 2-4 pieces of bacon in a pan until crisp. This can be done while the pasta is cooking. When cooked, chop up bacon and add to pasta when you combine the roasted cauliflower mixture.

8. Cauliflower Potato Soup

Serving: Serves 10 | Prep: | Cook: | Ready in:

Ingredients

- 2 tbsp (+ 2 additional teaspoons) olive oil
- 1 small (1 lb) cauliflower, cored, cut into small florets
- 1 small fennel bulb (reserve leaves for garnish) bulb cored and chopped
- 1 lb russet potatoes, peeled, cut into 1 inch chunks
- 1 large yellow onion, chopped
- 2 cans (14.5 oz each) chicken stock, plus 2 cans of water
- 2 tbsp kosher salt
- 1 bay leaf
- 1 tsp cumin
- ¼ tsp saffron threads, crumbled
- Freshly ground pepper to taste

Direction

- Heat 2 tbsp. of the oil in a large Dutch oven over medium heat; add cauliflower, fennel, potatoes, cumin, and onion and cook, stirring constantly, 4 minutes.
- Cover pot; reduce heat to low and sweat mixture 10 minutes, stirring once.
- Add chicken stock, water, salt, bay leaf, and saffron; bring to a boil, reduce heat to low, cover pot, and simmer 25 minutes, stirring several times, or until vegetables are very tender.
- Uncover; remove from heat and puree soup directly in the pot using and immersion blender or in a blender in 3 batches.
- Top with crumbled goat cheese or reserved fennel leaves.

9. Cauliflower Roast With A Nod To Ina

Serving: Serves 4 portions | Prep: | Cook: | Ready in:

Ingredients

- 1 medium sized head of cauliflower, broken into flowerets of equal size - about the size of a large grape
- 5 tablespoons good olive oil
- 1/4 to 1/2 teaspoons dried and crushed red pepper flakes
- salt and pepper - large pinches of each
- zest of half a lemon
- juice of half a lemon
- 3/4 cup chopped and toasted almonds
- 1/2 cup shaved or grated parmesan cheese

Direction

- Preheat the oven to 425 degrees. Place the cauliflower flowerets on a large baking sheet pan and spread so you have one layer. Drizzle the olive oil over the flowerets, and then sprinkle on the crushed red pepper, the salt, and the pepper. Use your hands to thoroughly mix the ingredients. Place in the oven.
- Meanwhile, assemble your other ingredients. After about 10-15 minutes, turn the cauliflower with a large spatula so you get an even roast on all sides.
- Allow the cauliflower to roast for a total of about 25 to 30 minutes, depending on how brown you like your cauliflower. Pull from the oven, and immediately add the rest of the ingredients. Toss thoroughly, and serve with additional lemon wedges or an aioli if desired.

10. Cauliflower Soup

Serving: Serves 4 | Prep: | Cook: | Ready in:

Ingredients

- 1 tablespoon ghee
- 1 tablespoon flour
- 2 teaspoons cumin seeds
- 1/2 teaspoon freshly ground black pepper
- 1 dash turmeric
- 1 bay leaf
- 1 tablespoon chopped garlic
- 1 tablespoon chopped ginger
- 1 carrot, chopped into small pieces
- 1 head of cauliflower, chopped into florets
- 1 quart veggie broth (or water)
- 1 handful cilantro, chopped

Direction

- Warm the ghee in a pot.
- Toast the flour for a minute, then add the cumin, garlic, ginger, bay leaf, pepper, and turmeric.
- When the flour is toasted and the spices release their fragrance, add the carrot, cauliflower, and broth.
- Bring the soup to a boil, lower the heat, and simmer until the cauliflower is very tender.
- Puree the soup in the pot directly with a hand-held mixer, or in batches in the blender.
- Season the soup with salt to taste and cilantro.

11. Cauliflower Soup With Coconut Milk & Chillies

Serving: Serves 4 | Prep: | Cook: | Ready in:

Ingredients

- 1 cauliflower
- 1 onion
- 2 garlic cloves
- 2 tablespoons olive oil
- 1 glass white wine
- 1 cup vegetable stock (water)
- 3 fresh chillies
- 2 teaspoons coriander seeds
- 1 teaspoon cumin

- 1 teaspoon nutmeg
- 2 teaspoons turmeric
- 1 teaspoon cinnamon
- 1 teaspoon fennel seeds
- 1-2 tablespoons fresh galangal(or 1 teaspoon dried)
- 1 fresh lemon grass
- 250 milliliters coconut milk
- salt&pepper
- fresh coriander leaves

Direction

- Clean and trim the cauliflower in small size florets. Cook them in a steamer basket until soft.
- In a dry heavy skillet, over medium heat toast the cumin, fennel and coriander seeds till they give off an aroma, stirring or shaking the pan often. Cool and grind in a seed grinder.
- In a large pot add olive oil, heat and add diced onions, mashed garlic, grated galangal, chopped lemongrass and the spices. Sauté for 2-3 minutes.
- Add the white wine. Reduce until half.
- Add the cooked cauliflower florets to the mix and pour the vegetable broth on top. Simmer for 10-15 minutes.
- Using a stick blender, blitz the soup until creamy and smooth, add a splash more water if it is too thick.
- Finally add the coconut milk and simmer for another 5 -10minutes. Serve with cilantro and chili slices.

12. Cauliflower And Mushroom Gratin

Serving: Serves 4 | Prep: | Cook: |Ready in:

Ingredients

- for the gratin:
- 3 tablespoons olive oil, divided
- 8 ounces crimini mushrooms, sliced
- 4 fresh sage leaves, minced
- 3 cloves garlic, minced
- 1 small onion, peeled and thinly sliced root to tip
- 4 cups cauliflower, cut into bite sized florets
- 1/2 teaspoon kosher salt
- 1/4 teaspoon white pepper
- 1/4 cup grated parmesan cheese
- 1/2 cup vegetable broth
- 1/4 cup cream
- 1 cup cherry tomatoes
- for the crumble
- 1/3 cup flour
- 1 tablespoon sugar
- 2 tablespoons butter, cut into 1/4" dice
- 1/4 cup parmesan cheese
- 1 teaspoon freshly chopped sage
- chopped fresh parsley for garnish
- additional small sage leaves for garnish
- 1/4-1/2 teaspoons fresh lemon zest for garnish, to taste

Direction

- Preheat oven to 400 degrees.
- In a small bowl combine the flour, sugar and butter. Use your fingertips to blend the ingredients together until they form small crumbles and holds together when you pinch some between your thumb and forefinger. Add the parmesan and sage and toss to combine. Set aside.
- Heat 1 tablespoon olive oil in a medium saucepan over medium heat. Add the mushrooms and sauté until they've given up their liquid and begin to brown, 5-6 minutes, stirring occasionally. Add garlic and sage and cook for 30-40 seconds until fragrant. Remove pan from heat and cover with a tight fitting lid - to steam and soften the sage and garlic, without browning. Set aside.
- In a large bowl combine the cauliflower and onions. Add the remaining 2 tablespoons olive oil, salt and pepper and toss to coat. Add the mushrooms and parmesan cheese and toss to distribute the ingredients evenly. Transfer the

vegetables into a small square or rectangular casserole dish, about 8" x 8".
- Stir together the broth and cream and pour over the vegetables. Sprinkle the crumble evenly over the gratin. Cover the gratin with tin foil and bake for 45 minutes, until cauliflower and onions are very tender. Remove the foil and dot the top of the gratin with cherry tomatoes. Bake for an additional 15-20 minutes until tomatoes pop and slump.
- While gratin is still warm sprinkle with parsley, a few small sage leaves and lemon zest. Serve.

13. Cauliflower, Brussels Sprouts & Crimini Sauté

Serving: Serves 4-6 | Prep: | Cook: | Ready in:

Ingredients

- 2 1/2 cups cauliflower florets
- 5 ounces sliced crimini mushrooms
- 10 Brussels sprouts, halved
- 1 onion, chopped
- 3 tablespoons fresh thyme leaves
- 1/2 tablespoon butter
- 1/2 tablespoon butter
- 1/3 cup lemon juice

Direction

- Toss the vegetables with the thyme and lemon juice in a large bowl. Set aside.
- Heat the butter and oil in a large skillet.
- Add the vegetables and cover. The vegetables should be in a single layer. Cook about 3 minutes or until just beginning to become tender. Uncover and cook, stirring occasionally, until all of the water evaporates and the vegetables are lightly caramelized.

14. Cauliflower, Snap Peas And Tomato Salad

Serving: Serves 6 | Prep: | Cook: | Ready in:

Ingredients

- Salad
- 3/4 pound snap peas, ends trimmed
- 1 cauliflower
- 1 - 2 tablespoons olive oil
- salt and pepper to taste
- 1 pint cherry tomatoes, sliced in half
- zest strips from 1 orange
- 1 handful dill, torn
- 1 handful cilantro, roughly chopped
- 1 handful mint, torn
- 1/4 cup toasted hazelnuts, roughly chopped
- Dressing
- 1 garlic clove, minced
- 1/2 teaspoon whole grain mustard
- 1 tablespoon Spanish sherry vinegar
- 2 tablespoons walnut oil
- salt and pepper to taste

Direction

- Heat the oven to 400 degrees. Bring a large pot of water to boil. Add the snap peas and parboil for 2 minutes. Drain and immediately plunge into an ice bath to stop the cooking process. When cooled, drain and spread on a clean tea towel to dry.
- Cut the florets from the cauliflower in uniform 2" pieces. Place on a roasting pan and drizzle with olive oil. Use your hands to coat all the florets with oil. Season with salt and pepper to taste. Arrange florets in roasting pan cut-side down, with plenty of space between florets. Roast for 10 to 15 minutes, remove from oven, turn and return to oven for 5 to 10 minutes, until florets are nicely browned. Remove from oven and set aside to cool.
- Make salad dressing by combining garlic, mustard and vinegar in a small bowl. Whisk in walnut oil and season with salt and pepper to taste.

- When ready to serve combine cauliflower, snap peas, tomato halves, citrus strips, capers herbs and hazelnuts in a large bowl. Toss with the salad dressing and transfer to a large serving platter.

15. Cheesy Cauliflower Casserole

Serving: Serves 4 | Prep: | Cook: | Ready in:

Ingredients

- 3 cups cauliflower floretts
- 1/3 cup white wine
- 1 tablespoon dijon mustard
- 1 cup shredded sharp cheddar

Direction

- Preheat an oven to 400 Spray a small 8x8 baking dish with cooking spray and break up the head of cauliflower and place evenly in the baking dish, set aside.   Using a small sauce pan bring the wine and mustard to a simmer for 5-7 minutes until it has reduced by half. Add in the heavy cream and let mixture simmer for 5 more minutes.   Stir in ½ cup of cheese.   Pour cheesy mixture over cauliflower, top with the remaining cheese and bread crumbs if you are using those. Bake 25 minutes until bubbly.

16. Creamy Cauliflower Puree With Fenugreek

Serving: Serves 6 to 8 | Prep: | Cook: | Ready in:

Ingredients

- 2 large heads of cauliflower, cored and cut into even-sized florets
- 3 garlic cloves
- 6 cups milk
- 1 stick butter
- 1 ½ tsps ground fenugreek leaves*
- chopped chives
- salt & freshly ground pepper

Direction

- In a medium pot, bring cauliflower, garlic, a pinch of salt and milk up to a simmer. Do not boil. Simmer covered for 12-15 minutes or until cauliflower is very tender.
- Strain cauliflower and garlic from milk mixture, reserving both. Melt butter with ground fenugreek in a small saucepot for 5 to 7 minutes.
- Puree cauliflower in a blender with 1-1 ¼ cups of reserved milk and melted fenugreek butter, working in batches if necessary. Adjust milk amount based on desired texture of the puree. Season with salt and freshly ground pepper and garnish with chives.
- *In order to grind the fenugreek leaves without any of the stems, place a small sieve over a paper towel. Add fenugreek leaves and crush the leaves between your fingers and/or against the sieve, itself. The ground fenugreek will fall through the sieve onto the paper towel.

17. Creamy Roasted Cauliflower Soup

Serving: Makes about 6 servings and doubles easily | Prep: | Cook: | Ready in:

Ingredients

- 1 nice size head cauliflower, broken into 1 to 2 inch florets
- 1/4 cup extra virgin olive oil plus 2 more tablespoons
- Salt and pepper for seasoning the cauliflower
- 6 whole cloves garlic, skins left on
- 1 medium leek, cleaned and diced
- 2 tablespoons butter

- 6 cups chicken or vegetable broth
- 1/2 cup half and half
- 2 cups cups shredded cheese (I used 1 1/2 cups Kasseri and 1/2 cup Parmesan but use whatever you like....Fontina, Jack Cheddar etc.)
- Croutons and parsley for garnish

Direction

- Spread the cauliflower florets on a large rimmed baking sheet, sprinkle 1/4 cup oil over, add a generous amount of salt and pepper and toss.
- Place the garlic cloves in a corner of the baking sheet and pour the 2 tablespoons of oil over.
- Roast the cauliflower and garlic in a 425F oven for 30 to 35 minutes until it lightly browns around the edges. At about the 15 minute mark, turn the florets with a spatula. Remove from the oven.
- In a Dutch oven or soup pot, gently saute the leek in the butter until it softens. Add the cauliflower and squeeze the garlic out of its skin into the pot.
- Add the chicken broth, bring up to the boil and then simmer for 10 minutes.
- Cool the soup to almost room temperature and then, in batches, puree the soup in a blender and return to the pot.
- Bring the pureed soup just up to a simmer, stir in the half and half completely and then slowly stir in the cheese a little at a time until it melts. Garnish each bowl with a little parsley and croutons. Soup's on!!

18. Crispy Parmesan Cauliflower Tots

Serving: Serves 4 | Prep: | Cook: | Ready in:

Ingredients

- 1 pound cauliflower florets
- 1/2 cup breadcrumbs
- 1/4 cup grated Parmesan
- 1 large egg
- 2 tablespoons chopped, fresh parsley
- 1/4 teaspoon garlic powder
- 1/4 teaspoon freshly ground black pepper
- Extra-virgin olive oil, for brushing

Direction

- Preheat the oven to 400° F. Line a baking sheet with parchment paper and brush with olive oil; set aside.
- While the oven is pre-heating, steam the cauliflower until tender, and cool to room temperature.
- Place the cauliflower on a clean dishtowel or piece of cheesecloth, roll up and wring to extract as much moisture from the cauliflower as you can.
- Transfer the cauliflower to a large bowl and break florets apart with your hands. Add the breadcrumbs, Parmesan, egg, parsley, garlic powder and pepper, and, using your hands, mix until mixture holds together.
- Using a tablespoon, scoop the cauliflower mixture onto prepared baking sheet. Use your hands to roll each scoop into an oval-shaped tot. Brush the tots with olive oil.
- Bake for 15 minutes, remove from oven, turn the tots over and brush with olive oil, and bake for another 15 minutes to crisp the other side. Serve warm.

19. Curried Cauliflower Flatbread

Serving: Serves 8 appetizers/4 main | Prep: | Cook: | Ready in:

Ingredients

- 1 medium cauliflower, 1/2 pounds, trimmed and finely chopped
- 3 1/2 tablespoons peanut, corn or grapeseed oil
- 1 cup whole wheat flour

- 1 1/2 cups light coconut milk
- 1 1/4 tablespoons curry powder, or to taste
- salt and ground black pepper

Direction

- Heat oven to 400 degrees.
- Put cauliflower in a roasting pan, drizzle with a tablespoon of oil, sprinkle with salt and pepper and toss. Spread into a single layer and roast until tender and nicely browned, tossing with a spatula halfway through, for a total of 15 to 20 minutes.
- While cauliflower roasts, put flour into a bowl. Add a scant teaspoon of salt and coconut milk, whisking to eliminate lumps. Batter should be about the consistency of pancake batter. Set aside.
- When cauliflower is finished roasting, sprinkle it with curry powder and toss; fold cauliflower into batter.
- Pour remaining oil into a 10-inch nonstick ovenproof skillet and put in oven. Wait a couple of minutes for oil to get hot, then carefully remove pan, pour in batter, spread it into an even layer and return skillet to oven.
- Bake for about an hour, or until flatbread is well browned, firm and crisp around edges. Check after 50 minutes. (It will release easily from pan when it is done.) Let it rest for a couple of minutes before turning it out and cutting it into wedges.

20. Curried Mustard Chickpeas And Cauliflower

Serving: Serves 4 hearty side portions | Prep: | Cook: | Ready in:

Ingredients

- Roasted Chickpeas and Veg
- 14 ounces can of chickpeas, drained and washed
- 1   cauliflower, cut into florets
- 1/2   broccoli, cut into florets
- 2 tablespoons extra virgin olive oil
- 1 pinch kosher or maldon salt
- black pepper, to taste
- Curried Mustard Dressing
- 1 tablespoon grainy mustard
- 1 tablespoon curried mustard (like Kozlik's)
- 1 tablespoon apple cider vinegar
- 1/4 cup extra virgin olive oil
- 1/3 cup parlsey, roughly chopped

Direction

- Pre-heat the oven to 425 F.
- Place the cauliflower and broccoli florets and chickpeas on a large baking tray. Sprinkle with the olive oil, salt and pepper, and toss to mix with your hands. Roast, stirring every 15 minutes for 45 minutes.
- While the chickpeas and cauliflower roast, prepare the dressing. Whisk together the mustards, apple cider vinegar and olive oil in a large, non-reactive bowl. Once the cauliflower and chickpeas are done roasting, add them to the dressing while they are still hot and toss to mix. Stir in the chopped parsley and season to taste.

21. Garlic Roasted Potato And Spinach (or Cauliflower) Curry

Serving: Serves 4 | Prep: | Cook: | Ready in:

Ingredients

- 1 White or red onions,chopped into small pieces.
- 4-5   Yukon Gold Potatoes,peeled and cubed.
- 1 bunch Spinach,washed and chopped.
- 3-4   Thai chili peppers (or 1-2 Jalapenos) cut longitudinally.
- 4-5   pearls of Garlic,minced or chopped into small pieces.
- 1 tablespoon Ginger Garlic paste,divided.
- 1 tablespoon Garam masala,divided.

- 1 tablespoon Cumin Powder, divided.
- 1 tablespoon Cayenne Pepper Powder
- 2 teaspoons Oil
- 1 dash Salt, divided.

Direction

- Add 1-1.5 tablespoon of oil to a pan and add ginger and garlic paste to it (The paste is available in most Asian stores. I make it myself, but blending equal quantities of ginger & garlic together). Sauté.
- Add the cubed potatoes, a dash of salt, a dash each of cumin powder, cayenne pepper powder, and garam masala to it and mix well so that all the spices coat the potatoes well. Do not cover the pan, we want crispy potatoes. Keep an eye on the potatoes and sauté occasionally so they don't get burnt. We want crispy, golden-brown potatoes.
- While the potatoes are getting cooked, add a teaspoon of oil to a pan. Add cumin seeds, ginger-garlic paste, Thai chili peppers, garlic and mix well.
- Add the onions and salt. Sauté the onions every now and then so they don't get burnt. When the onions turn golden-brown, add the spinach (or cauliflower) and mix well. I like adding spices in stages, so if you think you'd like more spices, add some now. Mix well. Cover and leave it to cook for a while. (Cauliflower might take a little longer than spinach to cook)
- When the potatoes are done, add them to the onion and spinach (or cauliflower mix). Garnish with cilantro and serve with naan, roti or rice.

22. Genius Cauliflower Soup From Paul Bertolli

Serving: Serves 8 | Prep: 0hours7mins | Cook: 1hours13mins | Ready in:

Ingredients

- 3 tablespoons olive oil
- 1 medium onion (6 ounces), sliced thin
- 1 head very fresh cauliflower (about 1-1/2 pounds), broken into florets
- Salt, to taste
- 5 1/2 cups water, divided
- Extra virgin olive oil, to taste
- Freshly ground black pepper, to taste

Direction

- Warm the olive oil in a heavy-bottomed pan. Sweat the onion in the olive oil over low heat without letting it brown for 15 minutes.
- Add the cauliflower, salt to taste, and 1/2 cup water. Raise the heat slightly, cover the pot tightly and stew the cauliflower for 15 to 18 minutes, or until tender. Then add another 4 1/2 cups hot water, bring to a low simmer and cook an additional 20 minutes uncovered.
- Working in batches, purée the soup in a blender to a very smooth, creamy consistency. Let the soup stand for 20 minutes. In this time it will thicken slightly.
- Thin the soup with 1/2 cup hot water. Reheat the soup. Serve hot, drizzled with a thin stream of extra-virgin olive oil and freshly ground black pepper.

23. Harissa Cauliflower With Mint And Aleppo Pepper

Serving: Serves 2-4 | Prep: | Cook: | Ready in:

Ingredients

- 1 cup olive oil
- 3 tablespoons dried mint
- 2 tablespoons Aleppo pepper
- 2 tablespoons tomato paste
- 3 tablespoons harissa
- some red pepper flakes (optional, depending on your spice tolerance and the heat of your harissa - taste first!)
- 1 teaspoon ground black pepper

- salt, to taste
- 1 head cauliflower, in florets

Direction

- Preheat your oven to 450 degrees.
- Mix together everything but the cauliflower in a large bowl and adjust seasonings to taste. Add in the cauliflower and make sure all of the pieces are thoroughly coated. Set aside for about 30 minutes.
- Spread the cauliflower on a baking sheet and bake in the over about 45 minutes, until soft and the edges are charred.
- Serve and enjoy!

24. Ina Garten's Cauliflower Toasts

Serving: Serves 6 | Prep: 0hours20mins | Cook: 0hours35mins | Ready in:

Ingredients

- 1 small head cauliflower (2 pounds)
- 4 tablespoons good olive oil
- 1/4 teaspoon crushed red pepper flakes
- Kosher salt and freshly ground black pepper
- 12 ounces Italian mascarpone cheese, at room temperature
- 6 ounces Gruyère cheese, grated
- 4 ounces thinly sliced prosciutto, julienned
- 1/4 teaspoon ground nutmeg
- 6 large slices country-style bread
- Paprika
- Freshly grated Italian Parmesan cheese
- 2 tablespoons minced fresh chives
- Flaked sea salt, such as Maldon

Direction

- Preheat the oven to 400°F.
- Turn the cauliflower upside down on a cutting board. Cut off and discard most but not all of the stems, then cut the florets into small, 1/2-inch clusters. Place the florets on a sheet pan, toss them with the olive oil, red pepper flakes, 1 teaspoon salt, and ½ teaspoon black pepper, and spread them out in a single layer. Roast for 25 to 30 minutes, tossing two or three times, until the florets are tender and randomly browned. Set aside to cool for 10 minutes.
- Set the oven to broil and arrange a rack 6 inches below the heat.
- Transfer the florets to a large mixing bowl and add the mascarpone, stirring to coat the florets evenly. Stir in the Gruyère, prosciutto, nutmeg, 1 teaspoon salt, and ½ teaspoon black pepper.
- Toast the bread in a toaster until lightly browned, and place in a single layer on a sheet pan lined with foil. Mound the cauliflower mixture evenly on each toast and dust with paprika. Broil the toasts for 2 to 4 minutes, until browned and bubbling. (Watch them carefully!) Transfer to plates and sprinkle with Parmesan, the chives, and sea salt. Serve hot.

25. Indian Stuffed Cauliflower Chappati (Gobi Ka Paratha)

Serving: Serves 6 | Prep: | Cook: | Ready in:

Ingredients

- 1 cup whole wheat flour
- 1/2 cup water
- 2 cups cauliflower shredded
- 1 onion, finely diced
- 1 teaspoon chaat masala
- 1/2 green chilli
- 1 teaspoon mango powder
- pinch chilli powder
- handful chopped cilantro
- 1 teaspoon sea salt
- 4 tablespoons olive oil

Direction

- Place the flour in a mixing bowl. Add the water gradually. Combine the flour and water to make a sticky dough. Grease your hands slightly with oil and knead the dough until it becomes elastic and soft. It should not be too sticky or too hard. To check, press the dough with your fingers-it should spring back if it is the right consistency. Cover the dough with a towel.
- To prepare the stuffing, mix together the remaining ingredients in the bowl, adding the salt right at the end (this to prevent any excess water forming- moisture is the enemy in preparing stuffed parathas!)
- Divide the stuffing into four portions.
- Now heat a nonstick frying pan or tava on high heat. Once the pan is hot, reduce to medium heat whilst you prepare the paratha.
- On a floured surface, shape the dough in to 6 round balls.
- Dip the ball in the flour and with a rolling pin, begin to roll so it becomes the size of a tea saucer.
- Place one portion of the stuffing in the centre of the chapati and join together all of the edges of the chapati so that they meet in the middle and press it down.
- Dip the stuffed ball in the flour. Take a clean plastic bag and lay it on the work surface. Begin to roll the stuffed ball on the plastic bag (this prevents the paratha from sticking to the surface).Roll gently until it is 7-8? In diameter.
- Increase heat of frying pan to high. Carefully pick up the paratha and flip from hand to hand to get rid of any excess flour.
- Place it on the frying pan. When it changes colour and small bubbles begin to appear turn it over and cook the other side. Brush the surface with a little oil and turn it over. Let it cook for about 30 seconds. Now repeat for the other side until your paratha is golden and crispy.
- Make the rest of the paratha using the same process. Keep them wrapped in a towel or foil.
- You're done! Best served hot with chilled yoghurt and pickle.

26. Korean Fried Cauliflower

Serving: Serves 4 | Prep: | Cook: |Ready in:

Ingredients

- Cauliflower
- 1 head cauliflower (cut into florets)
- 1 tablespoon cornstarch
- pinch salt, pepper & garlic powder
- For the batter and sauce
- 1 cup all purpose flour
- 2/3 cup cornstarch
- 1 teaspoon each baking powder & salt
- 1/2 cup ice cold water + 2 ice cubes
- 4 eggs
- 2/3 cup sugar
- 2/3 cup water
- 3 tablespoons gochujang sauce
- 3 cloves garlic
- 2 tablespoons sesame oil
- 4 tablespoons mirin

Direction

- or the batter: Whisk flour, corn starch, baking powder, salt, eggs, water and ice cubes in a bowl until incorporated. Let sit on the counter for 10 minutes until ice cubes are melted. The batter will be thick. This is good.
- Gochujang sauce: combine all sauce ingredients (sugar, water, garlic, sesame oil, mirin and gojuchang sauce) in a blender or a food processor and blend until smooth. Set aside.
- Or the cauliflowers: Sprinkles salt, pepper, and garlic powder and corn starch over the cauliflower. Add the cauliflowers to the flour batter, stirring to coat.
- In a heavy bottom skillet, heat oil over medium high heat. The oil should be high enough to cover the cauliflowers, about 2 inches. Working in batches, lift the cauliflower florets from the batter, shaking off excess flour. Drop the cauliflowers to the skillet and fry for a few minutes on each side, turning

occasionally until the coating is golden brown and crunchy. Remove and set on a plated line with paper towel.
- Let the cauliflowers cool down completely, at least 10 minutes before adding to the sauce. This will ensure the florets will be crunchy and not soggy.
- Add the cauliflowers to the sauce, toss to coat. Use a slotted spoon to transfer to a serving plate. Garnish with toasted sesame seeds and green onion. Serve

27. Lentil Salad With Roasted Radicchio & Cauliflower

Serving: Serves 4 | Prep: | Cook: |Ready in:

Ingredients

- For the Salad:
- 1 small head cauliflower, cut into small florets (450 g), see notes above
- 3 teaspoons olive oil, plus more as needed
- 1/2 teaspoon Aleppo pepper or freshly ground black pepper
- kosher salt
- 1/2 cup French green lentils, rinsed
- 1 bay leaf, if you have it
- 1/3 cup walnuts or more to taste
- 1 head radicchio, cored and chopped
- 1/4 to 1/2 cups coarsely chopped fresh tarragon
- 3 ounces goat cheese
- For the Dressing:
- 3 anchovy fillets
- 5 tablespoons extra-virgin olive oil
- 2 tablespoons minced shallots
- 2 tablespoons balsamic vinegar
- 1 teaspoon Dijon mustard
- 1 tablespoon fresh lemon juice, plus more as needed
- 1/2 teaspoon honey
- 3 tablespoons currants or more to taste

Direction

- Heat the oven to 400°F. Line a large rimmed baking sheet with parchment paper. Spread the cauliflower into a single layer on the baking sheet. Toss with 2 tablespoons of the oil, the Aleppo pepper, if using, and kosher salt all over. Add more oil if necessary. Spread into a single layer again and roast until the cauliflower is light brown, 20 to 25 minutes.
- Meanwhile, place the lentils, bay leaf, if using, and a few pinches of salt in a saucepan and add enough cold water to cover by at least an inch. Bring to a boil, then turn down the heat and simmer until tender, 20 to 25 minutes (or longer—sometimes mine take as long as 30). Add additional water if needed.
- Place the nuts in a medium sauté pan and toast over low heat until golden brown — keep a close watch! Transfer nuts to a board and coarsely chop.
- Meanwhile, in a large bowl, toss half of the radicchio with the remaining 1 tablespoon of olive oil. When the cauliflower is light brown, scatter the remaining undressed radicchio on the sheet and roast until the radicchio is wilted and the cauliflower is tender, 3 to 5 minutes more. Let cool.
- To make the vinaigrette, finely chop the anchovies and smash them into a paste with the side of a chef's knife. Combine with the remaining ingredients and whisk until emulsified. Add more lemon to taste.
- Drain the lentils well, discard the bay leaf, and transfer to the large bowl with the dressed radicchio. Toss the lentils, while they are still warm, with enough vinaigrette to lightly coat. Add a few pinches of salt.
- Toss in the roasted cauliflower and radicchio, 1/4 cup of the tarragon, and walnuts to the bowl. Toss with more vinaigrette until evenly dressed. Taste and adjust the seasoning, adding more lemon juice if needed. Add the remaining 1/4 cup tarragon if you wish. Just before serving, crumble the goat cheese over the salad and gently toss. Serve warm or at room temperature.

- Bake in pre-heated 350 F. oven until top is golden and crusty, about 40 minutes.

28. Macaroni Cauliflower And Cheese

Serving: Serves 4-6 | Prep: | Cook: | Ready in:

Ingredients

- 1 medium-sized head of cauliflower, divided into 1" florets
- 1 pound penne
- Salt
- 1 1/2 cups grated Gruyère cheese
- 1 cup grated sharp Cheddar cheese
- 3 tablespoons unsalted butter
- 2 tablespoons flour
- 1 1/2 cups whole milk
- 1 teaspoon Dijon-style mustard
- 1 teaspoon freshly ground black pepper
- 3/4 cup Panko bread crumbs

Direction

- Steam cauliflower until tender but firm. Remove from heat. Set aside.
- Bring salted water to boil in a large pot. Add pasta. Cook until just tender but still firm, 5 minutes. Drain and return to pot. Add cauliflower to pot.
- Combine cheese in a small bowl.
- Melt butter over medium heat in a small saucepan. Add flour. Cook, stirring constantly, 2 minutes. Whisk milk into roux. Cook, stirring, until thickened.
- Add 2/3 of the cheese to milk. Stir until smooth. Add mustard, 1 teaspoon salt and pepper.
- Add cheese sauce to the pasta and cauliflower. Stir to combine. Pour into a buttered rectangular baking dish.
- Toast breadcrumbs in a dry skillet over medium-low heat until golden. Remove from heat and toss with remaining cheese. Add a pinch of salt. Spread breadcrumb mixture over pasta.

29. Mushroom Pilaf With Cauliflower Rice

Serving: Serves 4-6 | Prep: | Cook: | Ready in:

Ingredients

- Cauliflower rice
- 1 medium cauliflower (about 2 pounds)
- 1 teaspoon garlic powder
- 1 teaspoon onion powder
- 1/2 teaspoon sea salt
- 15-20 saffron threads
- 3-4 tablespoons sunflower oil
- Mushrooms
- 3 tablespoons sunflower oil
- 4 cloves of garlic, minced or grated
- 1 pound mushrooms, sliced (I had mix button and oyster mushroom)
- 1-2 small sprigs fresh thyme
- 2 tablespoons chives, finely chopped
- 1/3 cup freshly chopped parsley
- 1/2 teaspoon sea salt
- 1/2 teaspoon freshly ground black pepper

Direction

- Cauliflower rice
- Cut cauliflower into florets.
- Mix garlic powder, onion powder, salt and saffron threads which you rubbed between the palms of your hands in a separate small bowl.
- First place oil over cauliflower and mix then sprinkle with seasoning.
- Roast at 400 F degrees for 35-40 minutes. Let slightly cool. In batches process in food processor till you archive consistency of the rice or any way you like.
- Mushrooms
- Place oil, garlic, mushrooms and thyme in the pan and sate for 3-4 minutes.

- Add chives, parsley, salt and freshly ground pepper. Keep sautéing until most of the juice evaporates.
- Mix cauliflower and mushrooms and serve.

30. Mustard & Cheddar Roasted Cauliflower

Serving: Serves 4-6 side dish servings | Prep: | Cook: | Ready in:

Ingredients

- 1 large head of cauliflower
- 3/4 cup mayonaise
- 1/4 cup grainy mustard (or any bold mustard) i typically use french's "bold n' spicey"
- 1/8-1/4 cups chicken or vegetable broth
- 1 cup shredded sharp cheddar cheese
- 1/2 teaspoon salt
- 1 teaspoon pepper

Direction

- Preheat oven to 400 degrees Fahrenheit
- Wash and dry cauliflower and cut into bit sized pieces (it's good to have stem and floret on each piece) and place into large bowl
- In a medium bowl, whisk together mayonnaise and mustard and slowly add broth until mixture reaches the consistency of thick yoghurt.
- Toss cauliflower with mayonnaise mixture ensuring that each piece is thoroughly coated (I usually mix it with my hands) and spread evenly over large baking sheet (you may want to spray the sheet first with non-stick oil)
- Sprinkle cauliflower with cheese and pepper and bake in oven for 15-20 minutes or until pieces are fork-tender and the cheese is brown and crispy
- Taste a piece of the roasted cauliflower and if you feel it requires salt, add to taste

31. Pizza With Roasted Cauliflower, Calabrian Chiles And Green Olive Tapenade

Serving: Serves 2 to 4 | Prep: | Cook: | Ready in:

Ingredients

- Green Olive Tapenade
- 1 1/2 cups pitted Spanish green olives
- 1/4 cup toasted almonds
- 3 anchovies, drained
- 1 Calabrian chili, drained and coarsely chopped
- 1 large garlic clove, coarsely chopped
- 1 tablespoon extra-virgin olive oil
- 2 teaspoons capers
- 1 teaspoon freshly ground black pepper
- Pizza:
- 2 cups cauliflower florets cut in 1/2 inch pieces, about 1/2 medium head
- 1 cup thinly sliced fresh chiles, such as Anaheim or Fresno
- Extra-virgin olive oil
- 1/2 teaspoon salt, or to taste
- 1 favorite pizza dough - enough for one large pizza
- 1 8-ounce ball fresh mozzarella, thinly sliced
- 2 tablespoons chopped Calabrian chiles
- 1/4 cup finely grated Pecorino Romano cheese
- 1 cup Green Olive Tapenade
- 1 teaspoon fresh lemon zest
- freshly ground black pepper

Direction

- Make the tapenade: Place all of the ingredients in the bowl of a food processor. Process to a coarse paste. (Tapenade may be made up to one day in advance. Cover and refrigerate until use.) Makes about 1 cup.
- Preheat oven to 500 F.

- Toss the cauliflower and peppers with 1 tablespoon olive oil and salt in a medium bowl.
- Thinly roll out pizza dough to desired shape on parchment paper. Lightly brush dough with olive oil. Arrange the mozzarella over the pizza. Spread the cauliflower and peppers over the pizza and scatter the Calabrian chilies on top. Sprinkle with the cheese.
- Slide the pizza and parchment onto a preheated pizza stone (or onto a baking sheet placed on the lowest oven rack). Bake until the cauliflower is tinged golden, the crust is golden brown and the cheese is bubbling, 13 to 15 minutes. Remove pizza.
- Drop teaspoons of tapenade all over the pizza. Drizzle with a little olive oil. Sprinkle with lemon zest and black pepper. Serve warm.

32. ROASTED CAULIFLOWER WITH SMOKED PAPRIKA

Serving: Serves 4 as a side dish | Prep: | Cook: | Ready in:

Ingredients

- 1 medium head cauliflower
- 1/2 cup canola oil mixed with 1 tablespoon smoked (or sweet) paprika
- 3 tablespoons tablespoons Panko (japanese bread crumbs) or non-GMO cornmeal for a gluten free version
- Sea salt & black pepper

Direction

- Preheat the oven to 430°F. Line a roasting or baking pan with baking paper. Cut the cauliflower into small florets – there are two ways 1) with your hands break and separate the florets into small florets or 2) slice the cauliflower widthwise with a knife.
- Put the florets into a roasting pan and pour over it the oil-paprika mixture. Sprinkle the bread crumbs or cornmeal, salt and pepper over the cauliflower and toss with your hands. The florets should be coated in the oil and bread crumbs.
- Put the pan in the oven and roast for 10 minutes – remove the pan from the oven and with a spatula, flip the cauliflower and put it back in the oven for 7 - 10, depends on the size of the florets. Roast until the cauliflower is golden-reddish and tender. Serve immediately.

33. Red Pepper And Cauliflower Chowder

Serving: Serves 3 | Prep: 0hours20mins | Cook: 0hours45mins | Ready in:

Ingredients

- For the soup:
- 1 tablespoon olive oil
- 2 cloves garlic, roughly chopped
- 1 small yellow onion, peeled and diced
- 1 red bell pepper, cored and diced
- 1 large russet potato, peeled and diced
- 2 cups roughly chopped cauliflower
- 2 cups vegetable stock
- 1 cup whole milk
- 1 bay leaf
- 1/4 teaspoon ground coriander
- 1/2 teaspoon ground cumin
- 1/4 teaspoon crushed red pepper flakes
- For serving:
- Grated parmesan
- Freshly ground black pepper

Direction

- In a large pot, heat a drizzle of olive oil on medium-high until hot. Add the garlic and onion and season with salt and pepper. Cook, stirring occasionally, until slightly softened, about 5 minutes. Add the bell pepper and crushed red pepper flakes and continue to cook until the pepper is softened, 5 minutes.

- Add the potato, cauliflower, stock, milk, bay leaf, 1/2 teaspoon kosher salt, cumin, and coriander. Bring to a boil, then reduce to a simmer. Cook, stirring occasionally and mashing a bit with the back of a spoon, 10 to 15 minutes, or until the potato and cauliflower are tender. Turn off the heat. Let cool slightly
- Ladle about 2/3 of the vegetable chunks and a little bit of liquid into a blender and blend until smooth (or use an immersion blender and leave some chunkiness un-blended). Be careful! This is hot! Duh. Return the blended soup to the pot; heat over medium and stir to combine, heating everything through.
- Serve the soup with black pepper and parmesan on top.

34. Roast Cauliflower With Raisins And Parsley Dressing

Serving: Serves 2 | Prep: | Cook: | Ready in:

Ingredients

- 1 cauliflower
- 1 bunch parlsey
- 0.5 teaspoons cumin
- 1 clove garlic
- 2 tablespoons Sherry vinegar
- 4 tablespoons olive oil
- 2 tablespoons raisins
- 1 teaspoon salt

Direction

- Rinse the cauliflower and cut into bite size pieces. (Reserving 1 large floret to make "crumbs"). Leave the florets in a colander to dry thoroughly or dry on a kitchen towel.
- Using your fingers, toss the cauliflower florets with olive oil and salt ensuring that every floret has a coating of salty olive oil. Upend the cauliflower florets into a large roasting pan, making sure not to crowd the cauliflower.

Roast for 30 to 45 minutes at 400 F until the cauliflower is soft and brown in parts.
- Steep the raisins in boiling water until they swell to double their original size.
- Finely chop the garlic and the parsley. Whisk the olive oil into the vinegar and add about 1/2 teaspoon of salt. Mix in the chopped parsley and the garlic.
- Take the reserved floret and finely slice to get cauliflower "crumbs". When you reach the stalk, turn the floret over continue until there is only stalk left.
- To assemble; arrange the roasted cauliflower on a flat plate, scatter over the raisins and the "crumbs" drizzle the parsley sauce on top.

35. Roasted Cauliflower & Avocado Salad For New Parents

Serving: Serves 2 parents plus 1 baby | Prep: 0hours10mins | Cook: 0hours15mins | Ready in:

Ingredients

- 1 small head of cauliflower, cut into florets
- 1/4 cup extra-virgin olive oil, divided
- 1/2 cup whole-milk Greek yogurt, divided
- 1/3 cup finely chopped herbs (see Author Notes), plus more on top
- Salt and freshly ground pepper
- 1 ripe avocado, cubed
- 3 ounces feta cheese, crumbled

Direction

- Heat your oven to 400ºF. Place your cauliflower on a sheet tray and drizzle with 2 tablespoons of olive oil. Don't season—salt isn't good for babies, so you'll season later. Roast for about 25 minutes, flipping halfway, or until golden brown and tender.
- In a mixing bowl, combine 6 tablespoons of yogurt, 2 tablespoons of olive oil, the chopped herbs, and 2 tablespoons of water. Season the dressing with salt and pepper to taste and add

more water if needed. Reserve the remaining yogurt for your baby to try.
- To assemble the salad, transfer the cauliflower to a platter, layer with the avocado and feta cheese, and sprinkle generously with salt and pepper. Drizzle with the yogurt dressing and top with more herbs.

36. Roasted Cauliflower And Potatoes With Bengali Spices

Serving: Serves 4 | Prep: | Cook: | Ready in:

Ingredients

- 1 medium sized head of cauliflower (about 1 pound), cut into medium sized pieces
- 3/4 pound red skinned or other organic potatoes (halved or quartered, depending on the size)
- 2 tablespoons oil (mustard or EVOO)
- 1 red onion, thinly sliced
- 1/2 teaspoon teaspoon turmeric
- Pink, regular or sea salt to taste
- 4 cloves garlic, sliced
- 1 teaspoon panchphoron (Bengali Five Spice)
- Crushed Red Pepper Flakes or Cayenne to finish
- 1 tablespoon chopped cilantro
- 2 tablespoons fresh lime juice (about 1/2 lime) optional

Direction

- Pre-heat the oven to 375 degrees.
- In a mixing bowl, toss the oil, red onion, turmeric, salt and garlic and toss and mix well. Place the vegetable in a large casserole dish (I find this works better than a baking sheet, even though it is spread out in both cases)
- Bake for about 10 minutes, scatter with the panch phoron and bake for another 8-10 minutes. The vegetables should be crisp and fork tender.
- Sprinkle with red pepper flakes or cayenne and the cilantro. Squeeze in the lime juice if desired and serve hot.

37. Roasted Cauliflower With Lemony, Garlicky And Capers Dressing

Serving: Serves 4 | Prep: | Cook: | Ready in:

Ingredients

- For the cauliflower
- 1 Medium size cauliflower
- Olive oil
- Salt and pepper to taste
- Lemony, Garlicky, Capers Dressing
- The juice of one lemon
- 4 Large garlic cloves, minced
- 2 tablespoons Capers, plus 1 tbs of it's brine
- 1/4 cup olive oil
- 1/4 cup Chopped parsley
- Salt and pepper to taste

Direction

- Pre-heat the oven to 375°F.
- The cauliflower is going to be roasted whole. Remove the leaves of the cauliflower, making sure that the florets remain intact. Wash the cauliflower and dry it. Place the cauliflower in a backing dish (I used a pie dish). Drizzle olive oil on top of the cauliflower and season with salt and pepper. (I would say I used about a table spoon of salt and pepper). Massage the oil, salt and pepper into the cauliflower. Place in the oven and roast for about 30 to 40 mins, until cauliflower can be easily pierced with a fork.
- While the cauliflower is roasting make the dressing. Chop the capers and add to a prep bowl. To the capers add the chopped parsley, minced garlic, the juice of one lemon, and oil. Mix until combined. Season with salt and pepper to taste.

- Take the cauliflower out of the oven after is roasted. Very carefully quarter it and poor the dressing over it while it's still hot.
- Enjoy!

38. Roasted Cauliflower With Spaghetti Squash And Crisp Prosciutto

Serving: Serves 6 | Prep: | Cook: |Ready in:

Ingredients

- 1   large spaghetti squash
- 1   large head cauliflower, cut into small florets
- 5 tablespoons extra-virgin olive oil, plus more for roasting cauliflower
- 4   slices Prosciutto, diced
- 1/2 teaspoon red pepper flakes
- 5   garlic cloves, peeled and sliced
- 1 tablespoon fresh sage leaves, chopped
- 1/2 cup grated Grana Padano, or more to taste

Direction

- Preheat oven to 375°F and place a rack in the middle of oven. Scrub the squash well and pierce the flesh with sharp knife all over. Place it in a shallow baking pan and bake in the preheated oven for about 1 hour. Let it cool.
- Increase the oven temperature to 400°F. In a large baking pan, toss cauliflower florets with a few tablespoons of the olive oil and season with salt and pepper. Roast until slightly brown and tender, turn them occasionally.
- In a large skillet heat 3 tablespoons of the olive oil over medium-high heat, scatter diced Prosciutto and cook until crisp and golden brown, about 4 minutes. Use a slotted spoon to remove prosciutto to a plate; set aside.
- Heat 2 tablespoons of the olive oil in the same skillet over medium-high heat and toss sliced garlic, red pepper flakes, and sage; stir and cook for one minute. Remove from heat, combine cauliflower in the skillet.
- Cut the squash in half lengthwise with a serrated knife; scoop the seeds and fibrous strings from the center of the squash. Gently scrape the inside of the squash with a fork to shred the pulp into strands. Place the pulp in a large serving bowl, add the garlic-cauliflower mixture, crisp Prosciutto, toss them together, and season with salt and pepper. Before serving, sprinkle grated Grana Padano on top of the dish.

39. Roasted Cauliflower With Tahini And Lemon

Serving: Serves 4 | Prep: | Cook: |Ready in:

Ingredients

- 1   large head of cauliflower
- 1/4 cup olive oil
- 1/2 cup tahini
- the juice of two lemons
- salt and pepper to taste

Direction

- Preheat your oven to 350 convection or 375 normal.
- Cut the head of cauliflower into bite sized florets and lay out on a baking sheet. Toss with olive oil and sprinkle generously with salt and pepper.
- Roast the cauliflower for 15 minutes, then remove from oven, toss it around. Roast for another 10 minutes, and toss again. After another 10 minutes it should be nice and golden. Remove from oven.
- In a bowl, whisk together the tahini and the lemon juice. If your tahini is very thick, add a little more lemon, or a bit of water. Pour the sauce over the cauliflower and toss to coat.
- Serve at any temperature.

40. Roasted Curried Cauliflower In A Mustard Thyme Cream Sauce

Serving: Serves 4 side dishes | Prep: | Cook: | Ready in:

Ingredients

- Roasted Curried Cauliflower
- 2 small heads of cauliflower
- olive oil
- salt
- black pepper
- curry powder
- Mustard Cream Sauce with Thyme
- 6 ounces amber ale
- 1 medium shallot, minced
- 1 teaspoon fresh thyme leaves, finely chopped
- 1 cup your favorite chicken broth
- 3/4 cup heavy cream
- 1 tablespoon Dijon mustard
- 1 tablespoon yellow mustard seeds
- pinch salt
- squeeze of lemon juice

Direction

- Roasted Curried Cauliflower
- Preheat the oven to 400F. Slice the cauliflower in 3/4" slices through the head top to bottom.
- Lightly toss on a baking sheet with enough olive oil to lightly coat the pieces; sprinkle with a couple healthy pinches of salt, pepper and one pinch of curry powder. Toss gently to coat without breaking the cauliflower into smaller pieces.
- Separate the pieces and roast for 30 minutes, or until tender. While the cauliflower is roasting, make the reduction cream sauce.
- Mustard Cream Sauce with Thyme
- In a medium pot over medium high heat, bring the beer, shallots and thyme to a boil. Simmer to until the beer is reduced to 1/4 cup.
- Add the chicken broth, bring back to a boil and simmer until the total liquid is reduced by half. You should have about 2/3 cup of liquid.
- Add the cream, bring to a simmer and reduce until you have 1 cup of liquid.
- Stir in the mustard, mustard seed and salt to taste. Finish with a squeeze of lemon to sharpen and balance out the flavors.
- Gently toss the roasted cauliflower with 1/4 cup of the mustard sauce. Serve some cauliflower on the plate and top with a drizzle of sauce.

41. Rustic Cauliflower Bake

Serving: Serves 4 to 6 | Prep: | Cook: | Ready in:

Ingredients

- 1 bunch cauliflower
- 2 tablespoons worcestershire sauce
- 1/4 onion, finely chopped
- 2 tablespoons ground mustard
- ground black pepper
- 1/2 cup sour cream
- 1/2 cup sharp cheddar cheese- finely grated
- 1 tomato- sliced
- 1/2 cup fine bread crumbs
- 2 tablespoons butter
- paprika

Direction

- Cook cauliflower in chicken broth until just tender. Use 1/2 cup chicken broth and 1/2 cup water.
- Mix together Worcestershire sauce, onion, ground mustard, black pepper, sour cream, and cheddar cheese.
- Fold this mixture gently with the cooked cauliflower until well coated. Place in a 2.5 quart baking dish. (Spray baking dish with cooking spray before pouring in mixture.)
- Slice tomatoes thinly and place over top of cauliflower mixture.
- Mix bread crumbs with melted butter.
- Sprinkle bread crumbs and paprika on top of tomatoes and cauliflower mixture.

- Bake in a 350 degree preheated oven for 35 minutes.

42. Sassy Moussaka With Cauliflower Parsnip Puree

Serving: Serves 8-10 | Prep: | Cook: | Ready in:

Ingredients

- Cauliflower Parsnip Puree
- 1 medium head cauliflower chopped coarsely
- 1 cup small parsnips chopped unpeeled
- 1 cup whole milk
- 4 ounces mozzarella
- salt to taste
- Moussaka
- 1 cup panko
- 2 tbsp butter
- zest of one lemon (with microplane)
- 2 tablespoons pine nuts roasted
- 1/2 cup Italian parsley finely chopped
- 3 tablespoons olive oil
- 2 cups chopped yellow onion
- 2 pounds ground beef or bison
- 6 cloves minced garlic
- 4 teaspoons ground vietnamese cinnamon
- 2 teaspoons freshly grated nutmeg
- 1 teaspoon ground cloves
- 1 tablespoon soy sauce
- 1/2 cup red wine
- 1 cup beef broth
- 1/3 cup tomato paste
- 1 tablespoon brown sugar
- 1 teaspoon vegetable bullion
- 26 ounces crushed fire roasted tomatoes
- 3 medium eggplant cubed 1 inch pieces

Direction

- Cauliflower Parsnip Puree
- Roast chopped cauliflower and parsnips in oven at 400 degrees until they are tender and slightly browned. Remove and let cool.
- Puree cauliflower, parsnips, mozzarella, milk and salt until smooth and creamy in blender. Add additional milk a little at a time, if needed, to create a creamy texture that is not runny or lumpy. Set this aside and cover-- reheat when you are ready to assemble the dish.
- Moussaka
- Melt butter in a skillet. Sprinkle panko over the butter and toast it until golden brown. Remove from heat and after it cools, toss with lemon zest, pine nuts, 1 tsp nutmeg and 1 tbsp. parsley. Set aside.
- Toss cubed eggplant with 2 tbsp. olive oil and roast in 400 degree oven until golden brown and tender.
- In another pan sauté onions in 1 tbsp. olive oil until translucent. Add ground beef, cinnamon, 1 tsp nutmeg, cloves, and garlic. Cook until beef is cooked through and browned.
- Add soy sauce, wine, beef broth, vegetable bullion, crushed tomatoes, tomato paste and simmer. Add remaining parsley just before serving.
- To assemble: Scoop approx. 1 cup beef mixture into a bowl. Sprinkle with roasted eggplant. Top with a large scoop of warmed cauliflower parsnip puree. Sprinkle with panko mixture.

43. Sauteed Tri Color Cauliflower

Serving: Serves 4 | Prep: | Cook: | Ready in:

Ingredients

- 1 head of cauliflower (preferably multi-colored), cut into florets
- 3 tablespoons Extra Virgin Olive Oil
- 1 clove minced garlic
- 2 anchovy filets, minced
- 1/2 cup Panko Bread Crumbs
- salt and pepper to taste

Direction

- Bring about 1 inch of water to a boil over high heat in a large pot. Throw in the cauliflower florets and steam for 2-3 minutes until slightly tender. Drain the cauliflower from the water and set aside.
- Over medium heat, sauté the garlic and anchovy in the EVOO for 1-2 minutes.
- Add the cauliflower and sauté for approximately 6-8 minutes, until slightly browned.
- Add the bread crumbs and toss for 30 seconds, then season with salt and pepper to taste.

44. Smoky Roasted Cauliflower And Celery Root Soup

Serving: Serves 6 hearty bowls of soup | Prep: | Cook: | Ready in:

Ingredients

- 1 head cauliflower (trimmed and cut into florets)
- 2 bulbs celery root (peeled and cubed into 1 inch pieces)
- 1 onion (diced)
- 3 cloves garlic, minced
- 4 cups low sodium chicken broth
- 2 bay leaves
- 1 tablespoon smoky hot paprika
- 3/4 cup cream or 1/2 & 1/2
- 1/2 cup freshly grated Parmesan cheese
- olive oil
- salt and pepper

Direction

- Preheat oven to 350 degrees. Put cauliflower on a baking sheet and coat with olive oil, salt and pepper. Bake in the oven for 20 minutes.
- While the cauliflower is baking, bring a large pot of salted water to a boil and toss in the celery root. Boil for 20 minutes. Drain and set aside.
- In the same large pot, heat olive oil over medium heat (about 2 tbsp.). Add onion and cook for 5 minutes. Add the garlic and cook for 3 more minutes. Add the bay leaves, paprika, salt and pepper and give it a good stir. Toss the celery root and cauliflower into the pot and cook for 3 minutes.
- Add the broth to the pot and bring to a boil. Add some more salt and pepper. Lower to a simmer and let cook for 5 minutes.
- Transfer mixture to a large bowl, remove the bay leaves, and run through a food processor in batches. Put the pureed mixture back in the pot on the stove over low heat. Alternatively, just use an immersion blender in the pot.
- Once all the mixture has been pureed and is returned to the pot, stir in the cream and Parmesan cheese. Add salt and pepper to taste. Serve with some crusty bread. Happy fall!

45. Squash And Cauliflower Salad With Cranberry Beans And Salsa Verde

Serving: Serves 2 | Prep: | Cook: | Ready in:

Ingredients

- For the Salsa Verde
- 2 whole pickled jalapeños in escabeche (I like Embasa brand)
- 3 tablespoons cilantro, finely chopped
- 2 cloves garlic, minced
- 3 tablespoons lime juice
- 4 tablespoons extra virgin olive oil
- For the Salad
- 3 whole yellow crookneck summer squash, cut into bite sized pieces. (Zucchini can be substituted)
- 12 ounces cauliflower florets, in bite sized pieces
- 2-4 tablespoons olive oil
- salt

- 1 cup cooked cranberry beans

Direction

- Combine all ingredients for Salsa Verde. Season to taste, and set aside to let the flavors combine.
- Preheat oven to 450.
- Toss squash and cauliflower in olive oil. You want each piece to be lightly coated in oil.
- Spread vegetables on a cookie sheet in a single layer, sprinkle generously with salt and roast until browned and soft — 20-30 minutes. Let cool.
- Combine beans and roasted vegetables with salsa verde. Serve at room temperature.

46. Sweet And Sour Stir Fry With Cauliflower Rice

Serving: Serves 4 | Prep: | Cook: | Ready in:

Ingredients

- 1/2 cup red peppers, chopped into bite-size pieces
- 1/2 cup onions, chopped into bite-size pieces
- 1/2 cup broccoli, chopped into bite-size pieces
- 1/2 cup peas, shelled
- 1 cauliflower head
- 1/4 cup vegetable broth
- 2 tablespoons soy sauce
- 2 tablespoons apple cider vinegar
- 1/2 teaspoon red pepper flakes
- 2 tablespoons water
- 1 tablespoon cornstarch
- 1/4 cup beet puree
- 3 tablespoons coconut oil

Direction

- MAKE CAULIFLOWER RICE: Wash the cauliflower and chop into pieces that will fit into your food processor. Make sure the cauliflower is completely dry. Grate on the largest grater setting in your food processor (or use whichever grater makes it look the most rice-like, I have the Breville Food Processor, and the large grate is so rice-like people don't notice it's actually not rice.) If you didn't fully dry the cauliflower before putting it in the food processor, then place it in a clean kitchen towel and squeeze out the water. Put in a steamer to steam for about 10 minutes on a low steam, then continue to try the rice every 5 minutes until it's cooked perfectly. You want it to be soft, but crisp, exactly the texture of rice. Cooking the rice perfectly is the key to this dish.
- STIR-FRY: Chop all the vegetables into bite size pieces. Put a glop of coconut oil into a wok. Begin with the onions, fry until a bit brown. Then add the broccoli, fry until they turn a bright green. Next add the peppers and peas, fry until finished.
- MAKE SWEET AND SOUR SAUCE: Add soy sauce, apple cider vinegar, beet puree, vegetable stock, red pepper flakes to a sauce pan and stir. In a separate bowl, dissolve the cornstarch in water. Add the cornstarch and water to the sauce pan and stir until thickened.
- FINISH: Take the sauce and pour into the wok. Be sure your stove vent is turned on because it will create a plume of steam. Mix the sweet and sour sauce with the vegetables.
- PLATE: Take two scoops of rice from the steamer with an ice cream scoop, then use the scoop to put the vegetable mixture on top of the rice.

47. Turmeric Roasted Cauliflower With Activated Charcoal And Goji Berries

Serving: Serves 6 to 8 | Prep: | Cook: | Ready in:

Ingredients

- For the turmeric ghee and the activated charcoal tahini:
- 1 pound unsalted butter, cut into 1-inch cubes
- 1/3 cup finely grated fresh turmeric or ground turmeric
- 1 cup tahini
- 1 tablespoon activated charcoal (like Solaray Activated Coconut Charcoal Powder), optional
- Lemon juice and salt, for seasoning
- For the finished dish:
- 2 heads cauliflower, cut into small florets
- 1 tablespoon olive oil
- 1/3 cup turmeric ghee (from above)
- 1/2 teaspoon salt, or more to taste
- 1/2 teaspoon black pepper, or more to taste
- 1 tablespoon activated charcoal tahini (from above), or more to taste
- 1/3 cup goji berries

Direction

- For the turmeric ghee and the activated charcoal tahini:
- For the turmeric ghee, place the butter in a medium saucepan and melt, stirring occasionally, until you see a thick white foam develop on the surface. When the butter starts to simmer, turn the heat to low and cook for 5 minutes without stirring. Then scrape the sides of the pan: The liquid should become clearer and brown milk solids should appear at the bottom. Keep scraping the pan. The bubbles should get larger. When the butter starts to develop a white foam on the surface for a second time, the ghee is finished.
- Take the saucepan off the heat, pour over a sieve, and mix the turmeric into the strained, pure butter.
- To make the activated charcoal tahini, pour the ingredients into a bowl and mix until well combined. Season with lemon juice and salt.
- For the finished dish:
- Heat the oven to 475° F and line two sheet pans with parchment paper.
- Coat the cauliflower in olive oil and ghee and season with salt and pepper. Distribute on sheet pans and roast in the oven for 10 to 15 minutes, until the florets are beginning to char.
- Lightly coat the cauliflower with the tahini, adding more to taste. Adjust for salt, pepper, and lemon juice, then garnish with goji berries and serve.

48. Vegan Cauliflower Alfredo Sauce

Serving: Serves 2 | Prep: 0hours10mins | Cook: 0hours15mins |Ready in:

Ingredients

- 2 cups cauliflower florets, chopped small
- 1 tablespoon garlic, minced
- 1/4 cup hulled hemp seeds or raw cashews
- 2 tablespoons nutritional yeast
- 1 cup plant based milk or water
- 1/2 teaspoon onion powder
- 1/4 teaspoon garlic powder
- 1/4 teaspoon white pepper
- 1/2 teaspoon salt
- 3-4 tablespoons fresh lemon juice

Direction

- Combine all of the ingredients except for the lemon juice in a pot over medium heat. Bring to a boil then reduce heat slightly to a simmer, cover and cook for 13-15 minutes until cauliflower florets are completely soft and falling apart.
- Allow to cool for about 5 minutes then pour the mixture into a blender and add in the lemon juice before blending until creamy.
- The sauce makes enough for two portions of pasta, or about 8 oz. of dry pasta and it will keep in a jar in the fridge for 3-5 days. Add to pasta right before serving.

49. Whipped Cauliflower

Serving: Serves 4-6 side dishes, depending on how big your cauliflower is. | Prep: | Cook: |Ready in:

Ingredients

- 1 Cauliflower
- 2 Cloves garlic, steamed along with the cauliflower
- 1 Bunch greens, any kind(optional)
- 1 teaspoon Curry powder
- 1/4-1 teaspoons Chili pepper flakes
- 1-3 teaspoons Horseradish
- 1/2-1 teaspoons Salt and pepper, or to taste
- 2 tablespoons Fat of your choice(butter, evoo, coconut or olive oil)
- 1/4 cup Sour cream or Greek yogurt.

Direction

- Cut up the cauliflower into florets and stems and core into roughly 11/2 inch chunks. Steam in a steamer basket along with the Garlic Cloves over boiling water about 20 minutes, or until fork tender.
- Meanwhile, put one tablespoon of oil or butter in a frying pan along with the red pepper flakes and curry powder. Stir over low heat until fragrant.
- Transfer cauliflower to the frying pan and lightly brown in batches if necessary. Then transfer cauliflower to your food processor.
- If using greens, wilt them in the frying pan, then add to food processor.
- Add garlic cloves and horseradish to food processor and 1-2 tablespoons of butter or fat/oil of choice, salt and pepper, and 1/4 cup sour cream or Greek yogurt.
- Process until smooth, scraping down sides of processor as necessary.
- Reheat, if necessary, to serve hot.

50. Cauliflower Shiitake Soup With Truffle Oil

Serving: Serves 6, 1 cup servings | Prep: | Cook: |Ready in:

Ingredients

- soup
- 1 tablespoon grapeseed oil
- 3 cloves garlic, chopped roughly
- 1 small onion, diced
- 1 teaspoon ground coriander
- 1/4 teaspoon ground nutmeg
- 1 large head cauliflower
- 1 cup chicken stock
- 1 cup whole milk
- 1 teaspoon kosher salt
- 2 cups whole milk
- 1 teaspoon ground coriander
- dash ground nutmeg
- toppping
- 1 tablespoon grapeseed oil
- 1 cup fresh shiitake mushrooms
- salt to taste
- small bunch watercress leaves
- drizzles, white truffle oil

Direction

- Clean the cauliflower and chop into small florets and set aside. In a soup pot, sauté the onions and garlic in the grapeseed oil. Once they are softened add in all the florets and sauté for 1-3 minutes, stirring them up from the bottom once in a while. Add in the stock and 1 cup whole milk. Cook on medium heat until it just starts to boil, being careful for it not to come to a rolling boil. Take the pot off the heat and using a hand held blender, puree the soup until no large visible chunks are seen.
- Clean and wash the shiitake mushrooms, cutting off and discarding the tough stem. Cut the mushrooms into long slices and sauté them in the oil for 3-5 minutes until they become small but before they turn crispy. Salt the mushrooms while they're cooking.

- To the soup pot, add salt to taste, additional measures of ground coriander and nutmeg and the remaining 2 cups of milk. Puree the soup with your hand held blender again to create further creaminess. Gently heat the soup for 1-2 minutes to serve warm.
- To finish, place a few watercress leaves, some sautéed mushrooms, and drizzles of truffle oil (a little goes a long way).

Index

A
Ale 3,15,18
Avocado 3,22

B
Bacon 3,5
Beans 3,27
Black pepper 5
Bread 26
Brussels sprouts 11
Butter 5

C
Capers 3,23
Caramel 3,6
Carrot 7
Cauliflower 1,3,4,5,6,7,8,9,10,11,12,13,14,15,16,17,18,19,20,21,22,23,24,25,26,27,28,29,30
Celery 3,27
Cheddar 3,13,19,20
Cheese 3,19
Cherry 7
Chickpea 3,14
Chilli 3,9
Cloves 30
Coconut 3,9,29
Couscous 3,7
Cranberry 3,27
Cream 3,4,5,12,25
Cumin 15
Curry 3,4,14,30

D
Dijon mustard 18,25
Duck 7

F
Fat 7,30
Fenugreek 3,12
Flatbread 3,13

G
Garam masala 14
Garlic 3,7,14,23,30
Gin 14
Gratin 3,5,10

H
Harissa 3,15
Horseradish 30

J
Jus 18

L
Lemon 3,7,23,24,29

M
Macaroni 3,19
Milk 3,9
Mint 3,15
Mushroom 3,10,19
Mustard 3,14,20,25

N
Nut 7

O
Oil 3,7,15,26,30
Olive 3,7,20,23,26

Onion 7

P

Paprika 16

Parmesan 3,4,8,13,16,27

Parsley 3,7,22

Parsnip 3,26

Pasta 3,4,7

Peas 3,4,11

Pecorino 5,20

Pepper 3,7,15,21,23

Pizza 3,20

Potato 3,4,8,14,23

Prosciutto 3,24

Pulse 6

R

Radicchio 3,18

Raisins 3,22

Rice 3,19,28

S

Salad 3,11,18,22,27

Salsa 3,27,28

Salt 4,7,12,15,19,22,23,30

Sea salt 5,21

Sherry 22

Soup 3,8,9,12,13,15,27,30

Spaghetti 3,24

Spices 3,23

Spinach 3,14

Squash 3,24,27

T

Tahini 3,6,24

Tapenade 3,20

Thyme 3,25

Tomato 3,7,11

Truffle 3,30

Turmeric 3,28

V

Vegan 3,29

W

Worcestershire sauce 25

Conclusion

Thank you again for downloading this book!

I hope you enjoyed reading about my book!

If you enjoyed this book, please take the time to share your thoughts and post a review on Amazon. It'd be greatly appreciated!

Write me an honest review about the book – I truly value your opinion and thoughts and I will incorporate them into my next book, which is already underway.

Thank you!

If you have any questions, **feel free to contact at:** *author@shellfishrecipes.com*

Alice Tinsley

shellfishrecipes.com